21 EASY SONGS FOR UKULELE

T0039683

Order No. AM1003893
ISBN: 978-1-78038-258-6
This book © Copyright 2011 Wise Publications,

Edited by Tom Farncombe.
Music arranged by Matt Cowe.
Music processed by Paul Ewers Music Design.

With thanks to David Courtney.

EXCLUSIVELY DISTRIBUTED BY

HAL•LEONARD® CORPORATION

7777 W. BLUEMOUND RD. P.O. BOX 13819 MILWAUKEE, WI 53213

banks of the ohio

Traditional

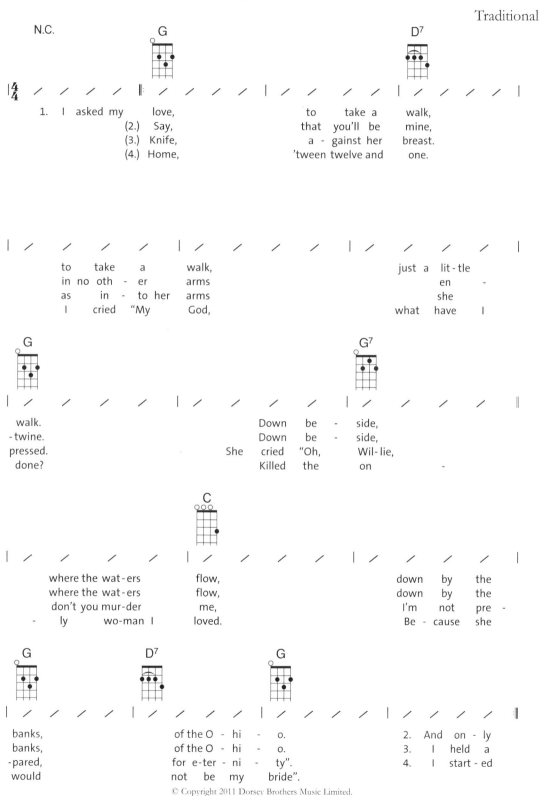

N.C.   G   D⁷

1. I asked my   love,   to   take a   walk,
   (2.) Say,   that you'll be mine,
   (3.) Knife,   a - gainst her breast.
   (4.) Home,   'tween twelve and one.

to   take   a   walk,   just a lit-tle
in no oth - er   arms   en   -
as   in - to her   arms   she
I   cried "My   God,   what have   I

G   G⁷

walk.   Down   be - side,
-twine.   Down   be - side,
pressed.   She   cried "Oh,   Wil-lie,
done?   Killed the   on   -

C

where the wat-ers   flow,   down   by   the
where the wat-ers   flow,   down   by   the
don't you mur-der   me,   I'm   not pre -
- ly   wo-man I   loved.   Be - cause she

G   D⁷   G

banks,   of the O - hi - o.   2. And on - ly
banks,   of the O - hi - o.   3. I   held a
-pared,   for e-ter - ni - ty".   4. I   start - ed
would   not be my   bride".

3

all my loving

Words & Music by John Lennon & Paul McCartney

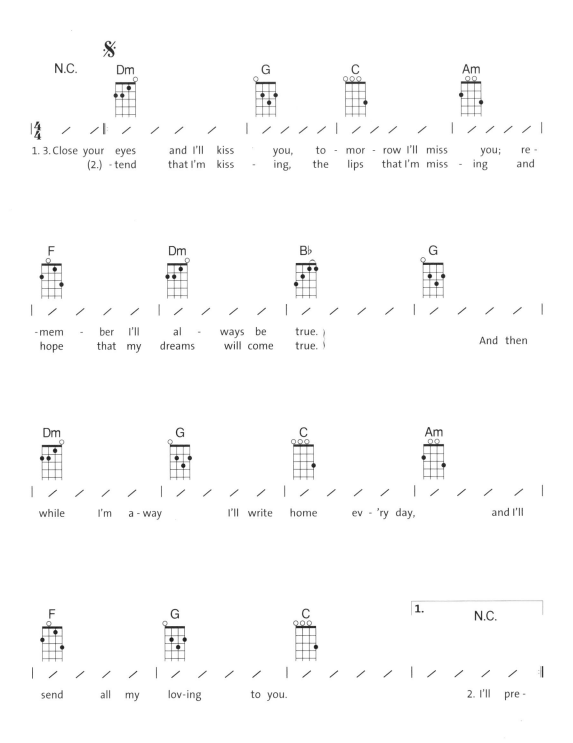

1. 3. Close your eyes and I'll kiss you, to - mor - row I'll miss you; re -
(2.) - tend that I'm kiss - ing, the lips that I'm miss - ing and

-mem - ber I'll al - ways be true.)
hope that my dreams will come true.)   And then

while I'm a - way I'll write home ev - 'ry day, and I'll

send all my lov-ing to you.   2. I'll pre -

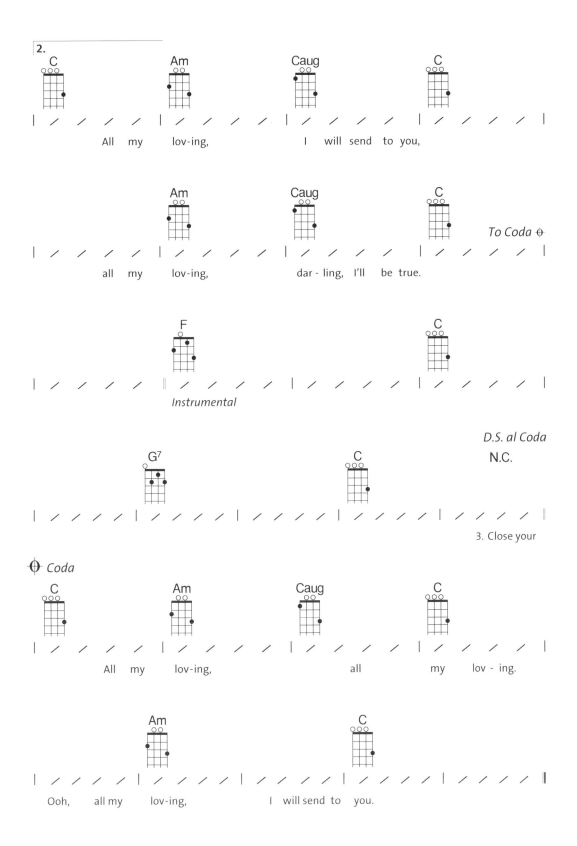

2.

C   Am   Caug   C

All   my   lov-ing,   I will send to you,

Am   Caug   C

To Coda ⊕

all   my   lov-ing,   dar-ling, I'll be true.

F   C

Instrumental

D.S. al Coda

N.C.

G⁷   C

3. Close your

⊕ *Coda*

C   Am   Caug   C

All   my   lov-ing,   all   my   lov-ing.

Am   C

Ooh,   all my lov-ing,   I will send to you.

all shook up

Words & Music by Elvis Presley & Otis Blackwell

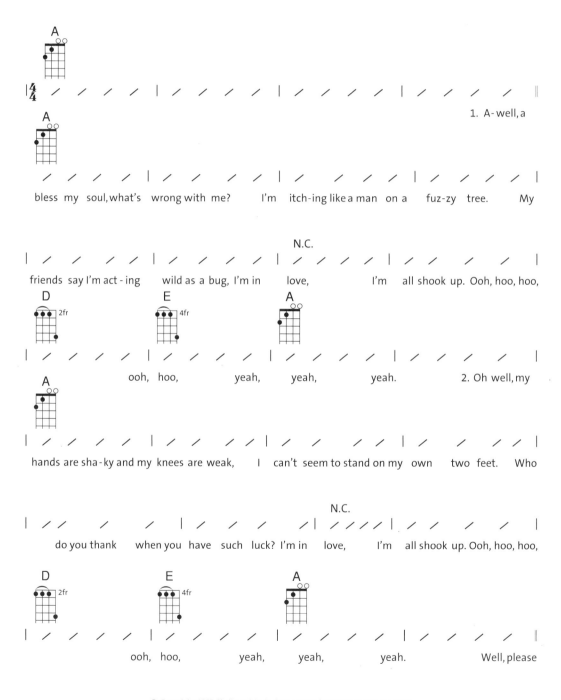

1. A-well, a bless my soul, what's wrong with me? I'm itch-ing like a man on a fuz-zy tree. My friends say I'm act-ing wild as a bug, I'm in love, I'm all shook up. Ooh, hoo, hoo, ooh, hoo, yeah, yeah, yeah.

2. Oh well, my hands are sha-ky and my knees are weak, I can't seem to stand on my own two feet. Who do you thank when you have such luck? I'm in love, I'm all shook up. Ooh, hoo, hoo, ooh, hoo, yeah, yeah, yeah. Well, please

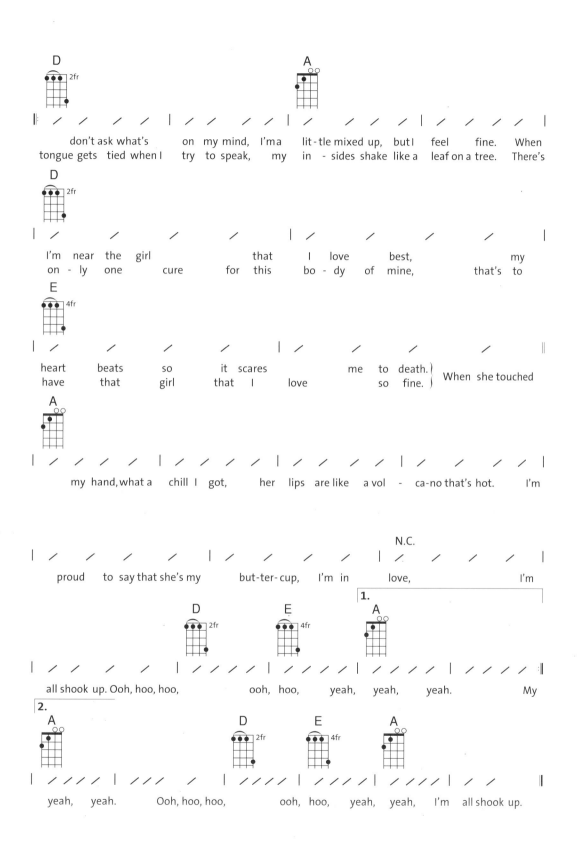

D   A

don't ask what's   on my mind, I'm a   lit-tle mixed up, but I   feel   fine.   When
tongue gets tied when I try to speak,   my   in - sides shake like a leaf on a tree. There's

D

I'm near the girl   that   I   love   best,   my
on - ly one   cure   for this   bo - dy of mine,   that's to

E

heart beats   so   it scares   me to death. }
have that   girl   that I   love   so fine. } When she touched

A

my hand, what a chill I got,   her lips are like a vol - ca-no that's hot.   I'm

                                                     N.C.

proud   to say that she's my   but-ter- cup, I'm in   love,   I'm

1.
                    D   E   A

all shook up. Ooh, hoo, hoo,   ooh, hoo, yeah, yeah, yeah.   My

2.
A   D   E   A

yeah, yeah.   Ooh, hoo, hoo,   ooh, hoo, yeah, yeah, I'm all shook up.

blowin' in the wind

Words & Music by Bob Dylan

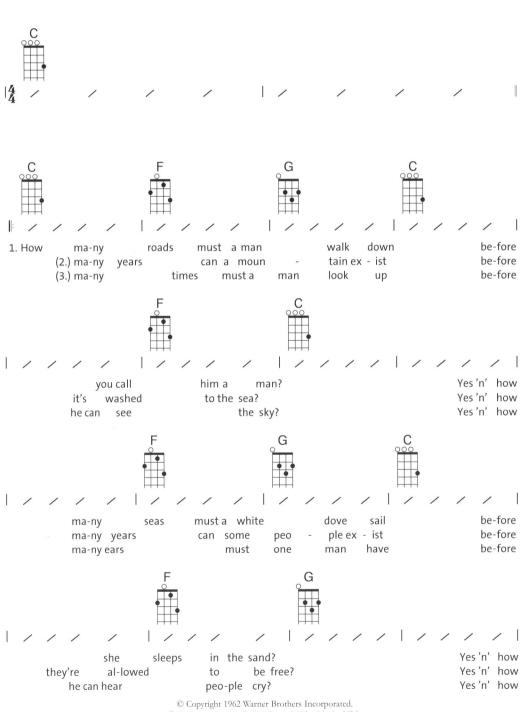

1. How   ma-ny   roads   must a man   walk   down   be-fore
(2.) ma-ny   years   can a moun   -   tain ex - ist   be-fore
(3.) ma-ny   times   must a   man   look   up   be-fore

you call   him a   man?   Yes 'n' how
it's   washed   to the sea?   Yes 'n' how
he can   see   the sky?   Yes 'n' how

ma-ny   seas   must a white   dove   sail   be-fore
ma-ny years   can some   peo   -   ple ex - ist   be-fore
ma-ny ears   must   one   man   have   be-fore

she   sleeps   in the sand?   Yes 'n' how
they're   al-lowed   to   be free?   Yes 'n' how
he can hear   peo-ple   cry?   Yes 'n' how

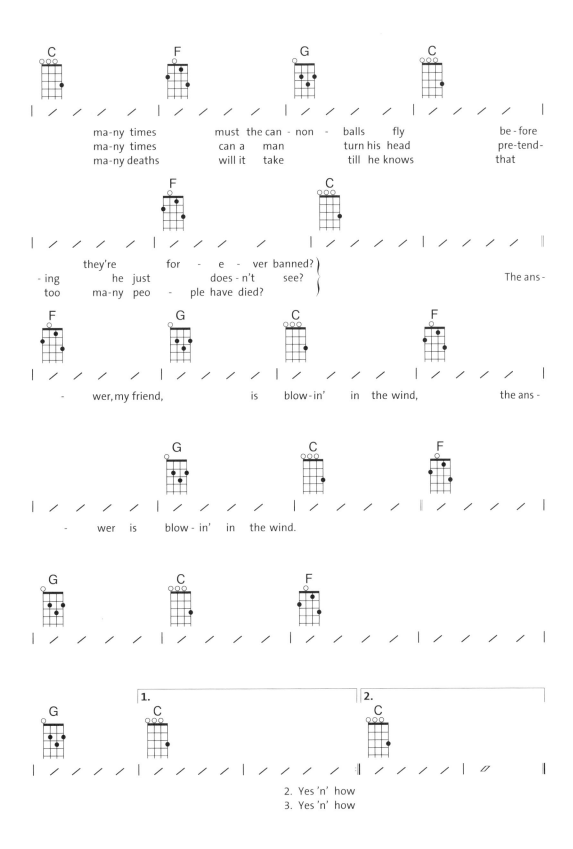

C   F   G   C

| ╱ ╱ ╱ | ╱ ╱ ╱ | ╱ ╱ ╱ | ╱ ╱ ╱ |

ma-ny times   must the can - non - balls   fly   be - fore
ma-ny times   can a   man   turn his head   pre-tend-
ma-ny deaths   will it   take   till he knows   that

F   C

| ╱ ╱ ╱ | ╱ ╱ ╱ | ╱ ╱ ╱ | ╱ ╱ ╱ ‖

they're   for - e - ver banned? ⎫
- ing   he just   does - n't   see? ⎬   The ans-
too   ma-ny peo - ple have died? ⎭

F   G   C   F

| ╱ ╱ ╱ | ╱ ╱ ╱ | ╱ ╱ ╱ | ╱ ╱ ╱ |

- wer, my friend,   is   blow-in'   in   the wind,   the ans -

G   C   F

| ╱ ╱ ╱ | ╱ ╱ ╱ | ╱ ╱ ╱ ‖ ╱ ╱ ╱ |

- wer   is   blow - in'   in   the wind.

G   C   F

| ╱ ╱ ╱ | ╱ ╱ ╱ | ╱ ╱ ╱ | ╱ ╱ ╱ |

1.   **2.**

G   C   C

| ╱ ╱ ╱ | ╱ ╱ ╱ | ╱ ╱ ╱ ‖ ╱ ╱ | ⫽ |

2. Yes 'n' how
3. Yes 'n' how

9

blue suede shoes

Words & Music by Carl Lee Perkins

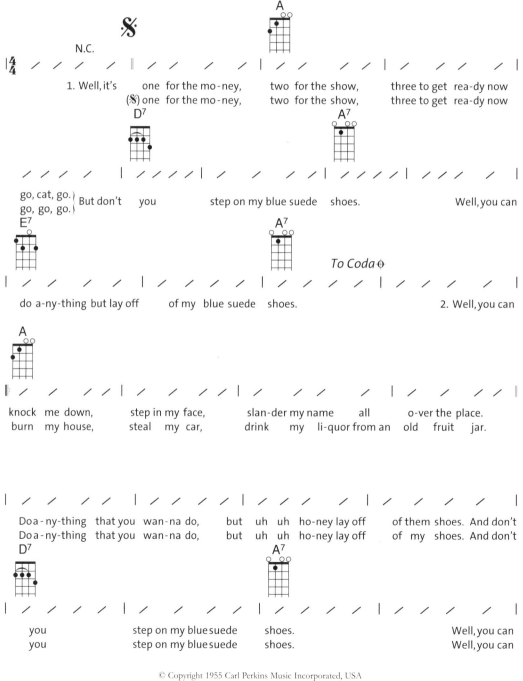

1. Well, it's one for the mo-ney, two for the show, three to get rea-dy now
(%) one for the mo-ney, two for the show, three to get rea-dy now

go, cat, go. }
go, go, go. } But don't you step on my blue suede shoes. Well, you can

do a-ny-thing but lay off of my blue suede shoes. 2. Well, you can

knock me down, step in my face, slan-der my name all o-ver the place.
burn my house, steal my car, drink my li-quor from an old fruit jar.

Do a-ny-thing that you wan-na do, but uh uh ho-ney lay off of them shoes. And don't
Do a-ny-thing that you wan-na do, but uh uh ho-ney lay off of my shoes. And don't

you step on my blue suede shoes. Well, you can
you step on my blue suede shoes. Well, you can

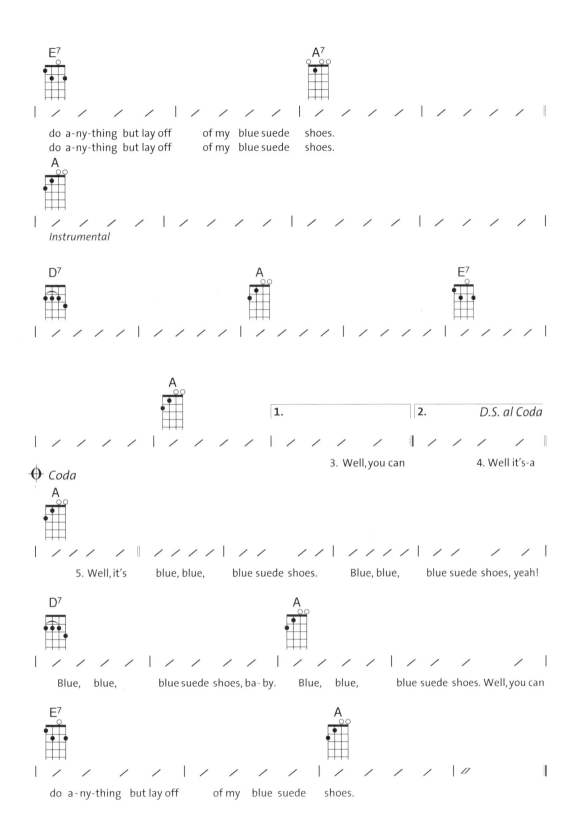

E⁷   A⁷

| / / / / | / / / / | / / / / | / / / / ‖

do a-ny-thing but lay off   of my   blue suede   shoes.
do a-ny-thing but lay off   of my   blue suede   shoes.

A

| / / / / | / / / / | / / / / | / / / / |

Instrumental

D⁷   A   E⁷

| / / / / | / / / / | / / / / | / / / / | / / / / |

A

                                1.   2.   *D.S. al Coda*

| / / / / | / / / / | / / / / ‖ / / / / ‖

                              3. Well, you can   4. Well it's-a

✠ *Coda*

A

| / / / / ‖ / / / / | / / / / | / / / / | / / / / |

      5. Well, it's   blue, blue,   blue suede shoes.   Blue, blue,   blue suede shoes, yeah!

D⁷   A

| / / / / | / / / / | / / / / | / |

Blue,   blue,   blue suede shoes, ba-by.   Blue,   blue,   blue suede shoes. Well, you can

E⁷   A

| / / / / | / / / / | / / / / | 𝄎 ‖

do a-ny-thing but lay off   of my   blue suede   shoes.

bring me sunshine

Words by Sylvia Dee
Music by Arthur Kent

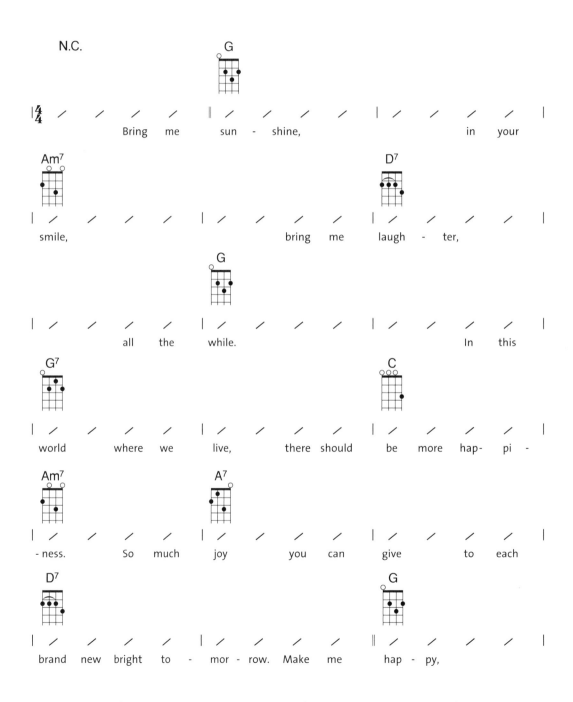

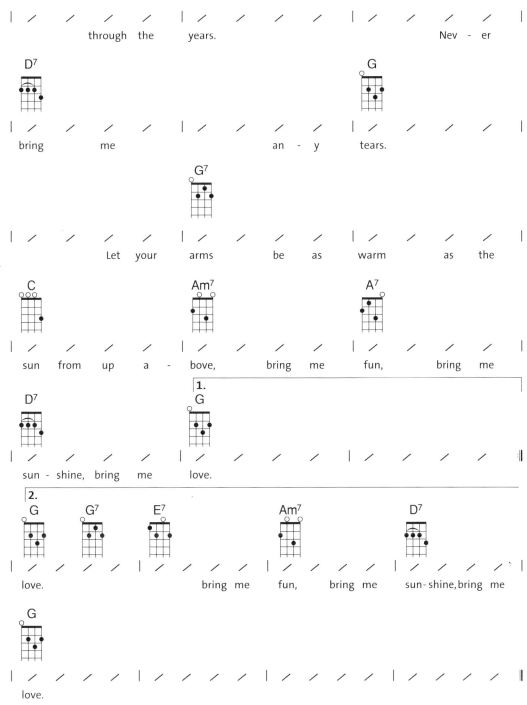

through the   years.   Nev - er

bring   me   an - y   tears.

Let   your   arms   be   as   warm   as   the

sun   from   up   a -   bove,   bring   me   fun,   bring   me

1.

sun - shine,   bring   me   love.

2.

love.   bring   me   fun,   bring   me   sun-shine,bring   me

love.

bye bye love

Words & Music by Felice Bryant & Boudleaux Bryant

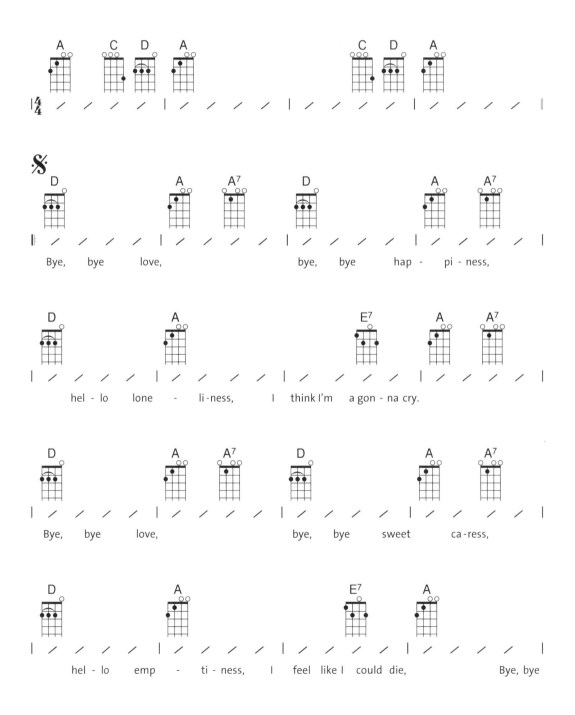

Bye, bye love, bye, bye hap - pi - ness,

hel - lo lone - li - ness, I think I'm a gon - na cry.

Bye, bye love, bye, bye sweet ca - ress,

hel - lo emp - ti - ness, I feel like I could die, Bye, bye

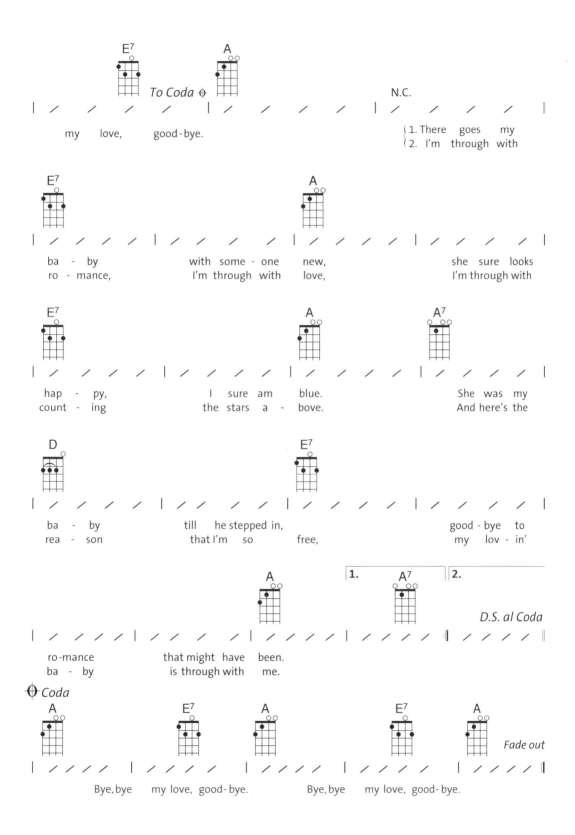

crocodile rock

Words & Music by Elton John & Bernie Taupin

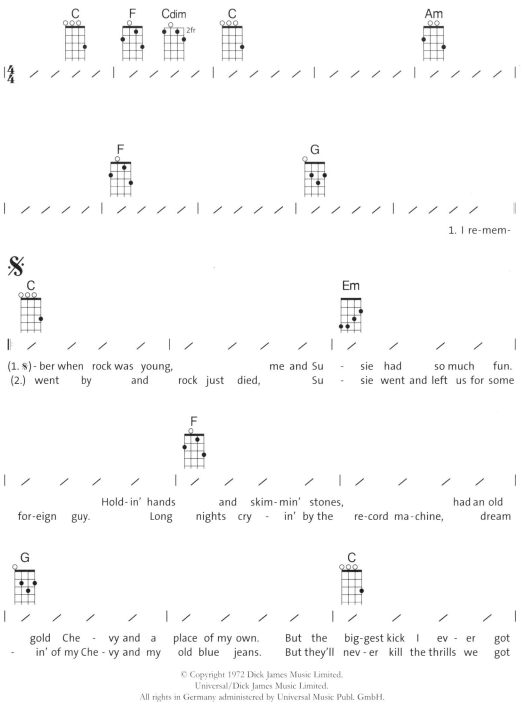

1. I re-mem-

(1. %)- ber when rock was young,   me and Su - sie had   so much fun.
(2.) went   by   and   rock just died,   Su - sie went and left us for some

         Hold - in' hands   and skim - min' stones,   had an old
for - eign guy.   Long   nights cry - in' by the re - cord ma - chine,   dream

         gold Che - vy and a   place of my own. But the big-gest kick I ev - er got
- in' of my Che - vy and my old blue jeans. But they'll nev - er kill the thrills we got

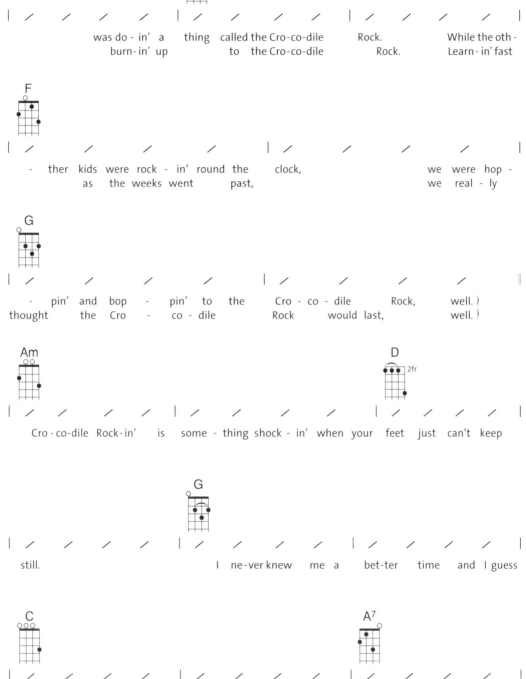

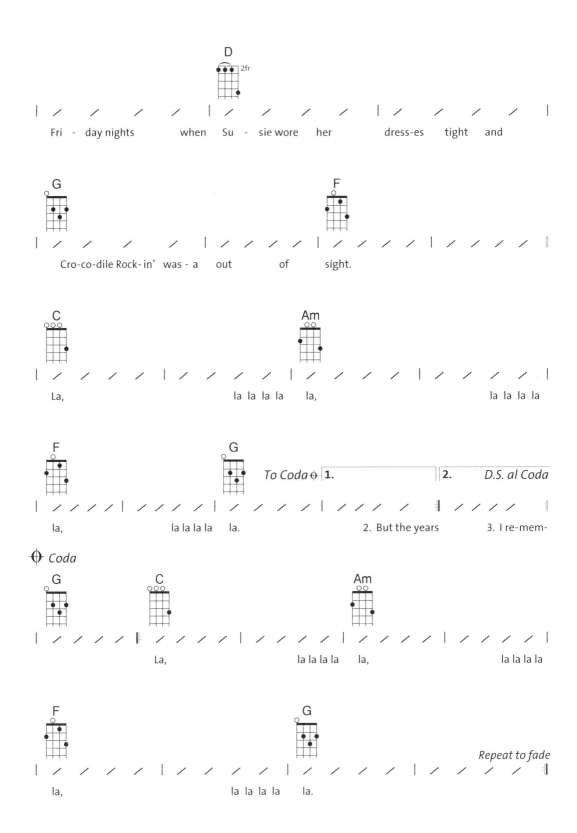

18

delilah

Words & Music by Les Reed & Barry Mason

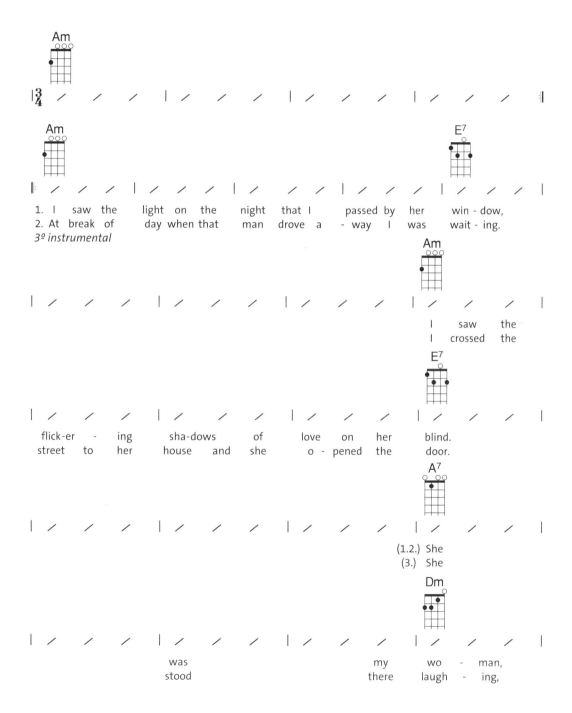

1. I saw the   light on the   night that I   passed by her   win - dow,
2. At break of   day when that   man drove a - way I   was   wait - ing.
3º instrumental

I   saw the
I   crossed the

flick-er - ing   sha-dows   of   love   on her   blind.
street   to her   house   and   she   o - pened the   door.

(1.2.) She
(3.) She

was   my   wo - man,
stood   there   laugh - ing,

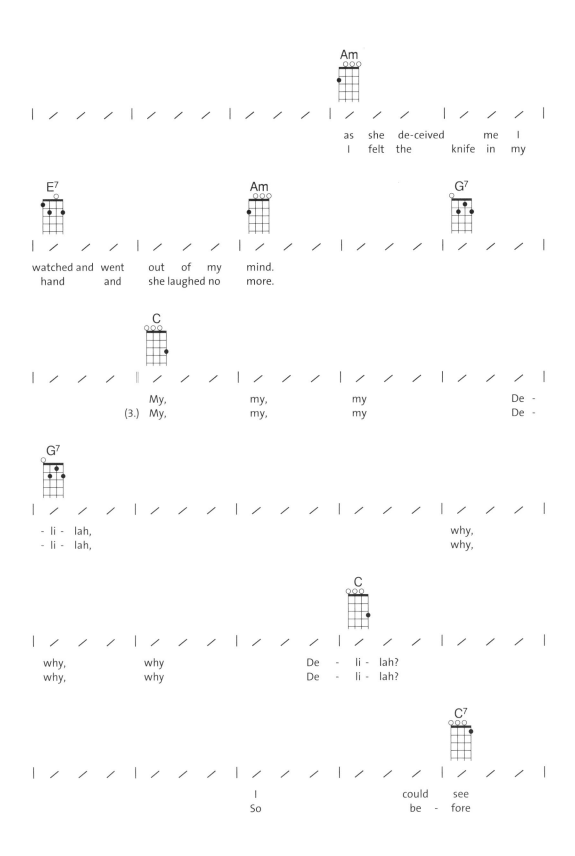

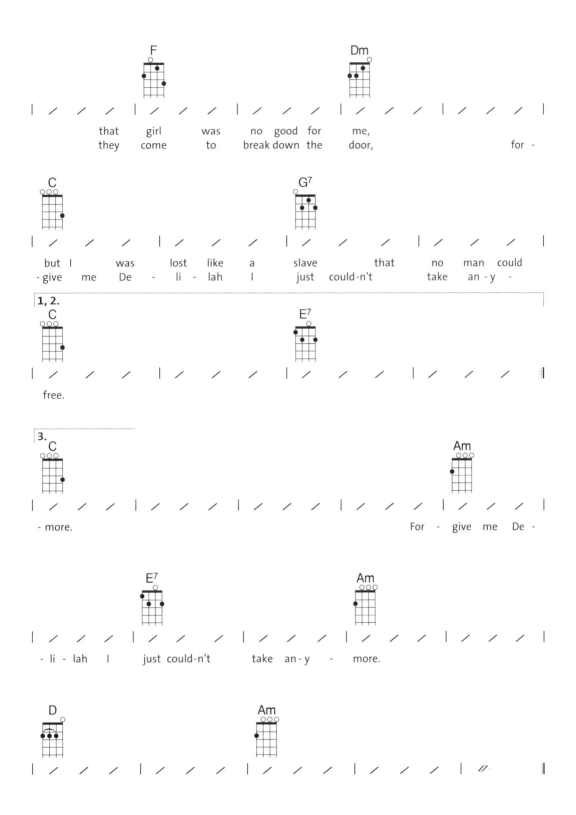

that girl was no good for me,
they come to break down the door, for -

but I was lost like a slave that no man could
-give me De - li - lah I just could-n't take an - y -

1, 2.

free.

-more. For - give me De -

-li - lah I just could-n't take an - y - more.

eight days a week

Words & Music by John Lennon & Paul McCartney

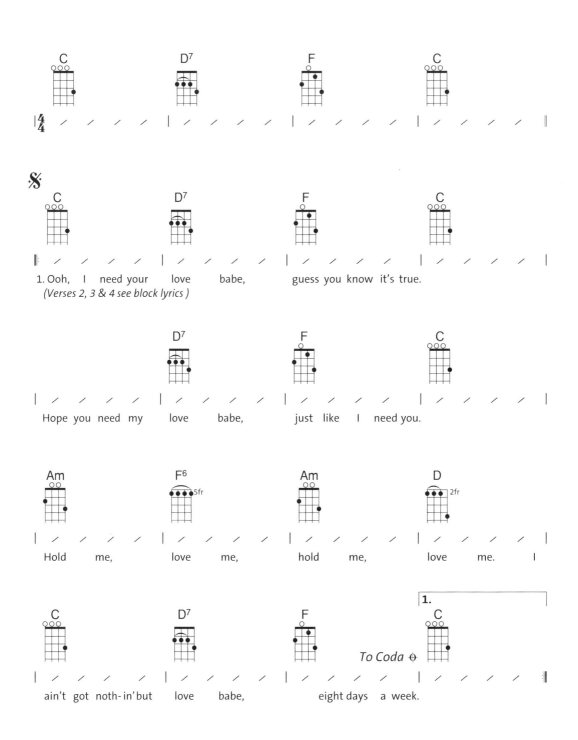

1. Ooh, I need your love babe, guess you know it's true.
(Verses 2, 3 & 4 see block lyrics)

Hope you need my love babe, just like I need you.

Hold me, love me, hold me, love me. I

ain't got noth-in' but love babe, eight days a week.

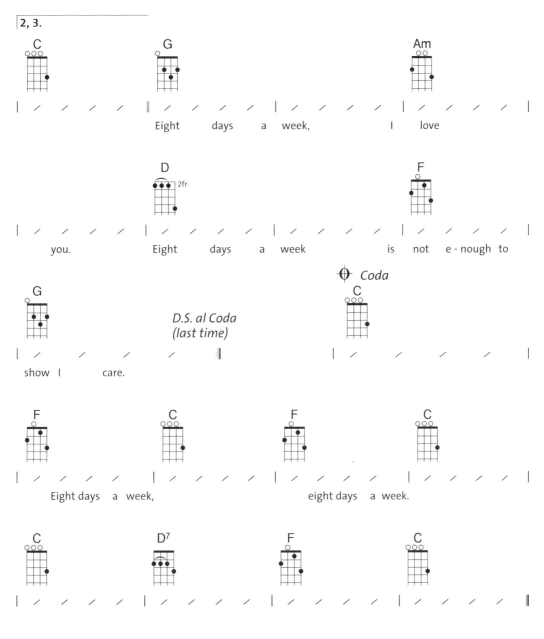

2, 3.

C   G   Am

Eight   days   a   week,   I   love

D (2fr)   F

you.   Eight   days   a   week   is   not   e-nough   to

⊕ *Coda*

G   *D.S. al Coda (last time)*   C

show   I   care.

F   C   F   C

Eight days   a   week,   eight days   a   week.

C   D⁷   F   C

Verse 2
Love you every day girl, always on my mind.
One thing I can say girl, love you all the time.
Hold me, love me, hold me, love me.
I ain't got nothin' but love, girl, eight days a week.

Verse 3
Ooh, I need your love babe, guess you know it's true.
Hope you need my love babe, just like I need you.
Hold me, love me, hold me, love me.
I ain't got nothin' but love, girl, eight days a week.

Verse 4
Love you every day girl, always on my mind.
One thing I can say girl, love you all the time.
Hold me, love me, hold me, love me.
I ain't got nothin' but love, babe, eight days a week.

everyday

Words & Music by Charles Hardin & Norman Petty

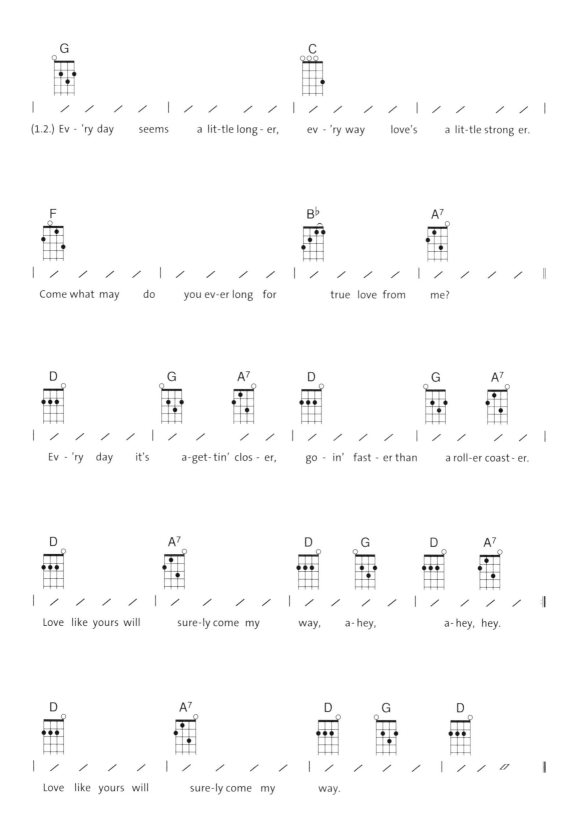

G   C

| / / / / | / / / / | / / / / | / / / / |

(1.2.) Ev - 'ry day   seems   a lit-tle long - er,   ev - 'ry way   love's   a lit-tle strong er.

F   B♭   A⁷

| / / / / | / / / / | / / / / | / / / / ‖

Come what may   do   you ev-er long for   true love from   me?

D   G   A⁷   D   G   A⁷

| / / / / | / / / / | / / / / | / / / / |

Ev - 'ry day   it's   a-get-tin' clos - er,   go - in' fast - er than   a roll-er coast - er.

D   A⁷   D   G   D   A⁷

| / / / / | / / / / | / / / / | / / / / ‖

Love like yours will   sure-ly come my   way,   a-hey,   a-hey, hey.

D   A⁷   D   G   D

| / / / / | / / / / | / / / / | / / // ‖

Love like yours will   sure-ly come my   way.

get back

Words & Music by John Lennon & Paul McCartney

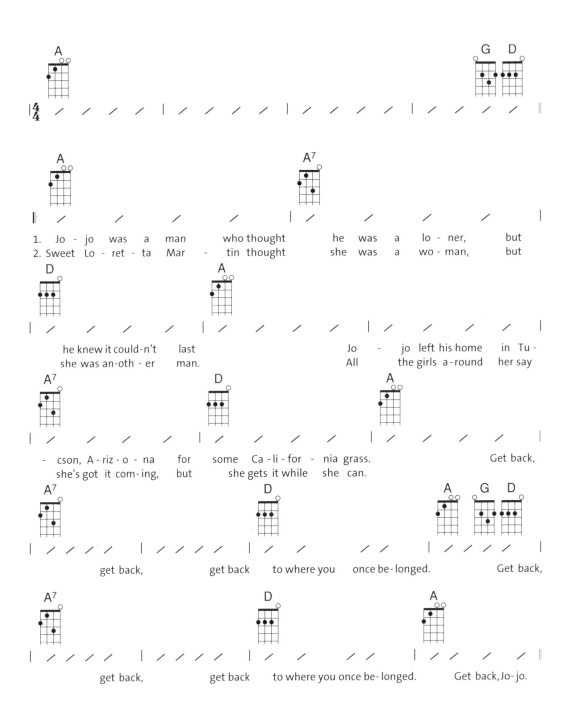

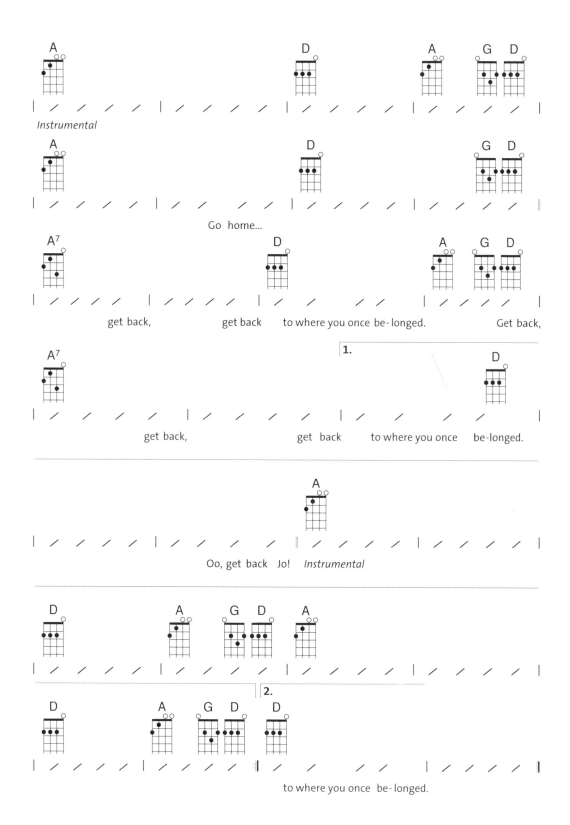

27

i'm a believer

Words & Music by Neil Diamond

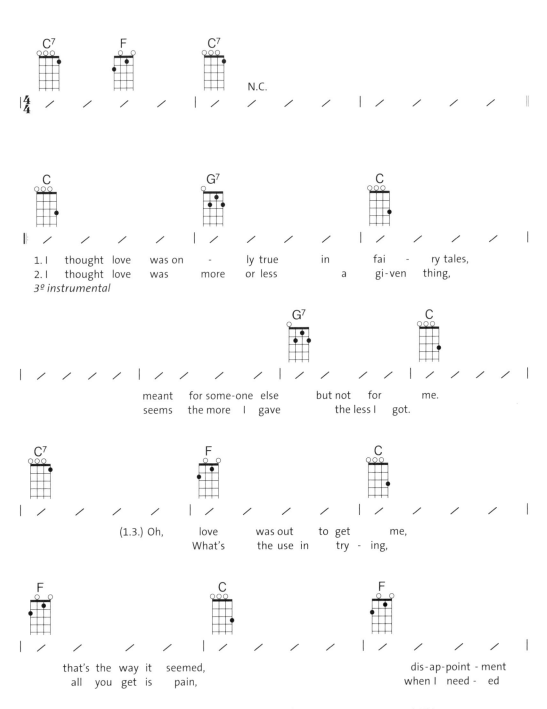

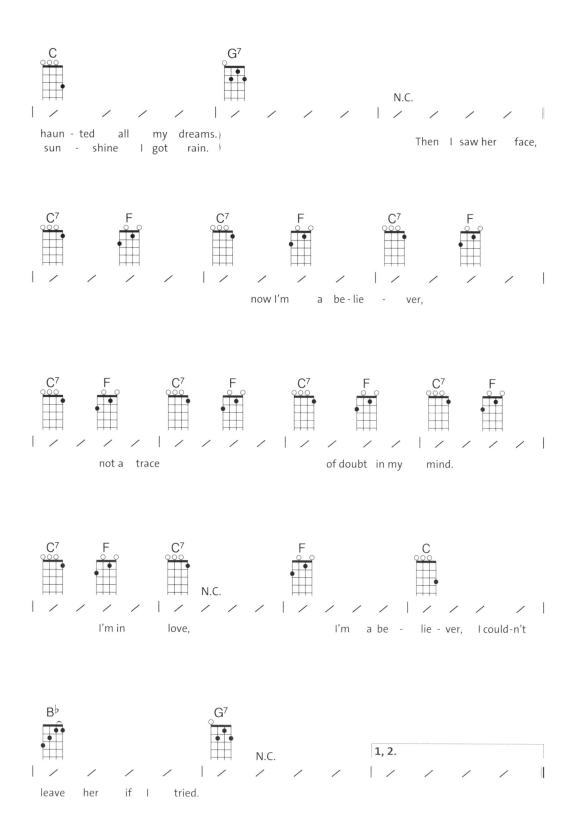

C   G⁷   N.C.

haun - ted   all   my   dreams.
sun - shine   I got   rain.   Then I saw her   face,

C⁷   F   C⁷   F   C⁷   F

now I'm   a be - lie - ver,

C⁷   F   C⁷   F   C⁷   F   C⁷   F

not a   trace   of doubt in my   mind.

C⁷   F   C⁷   F   C
                         N.C.

I'm in   love,   I'm a be - lie - ver, I could-n't

B♭   G⁷   1, 2.
                                            N.C.

leave   her   if I   tried.

it's not unusual

Words & Music by Gordon Mills & Les Reed

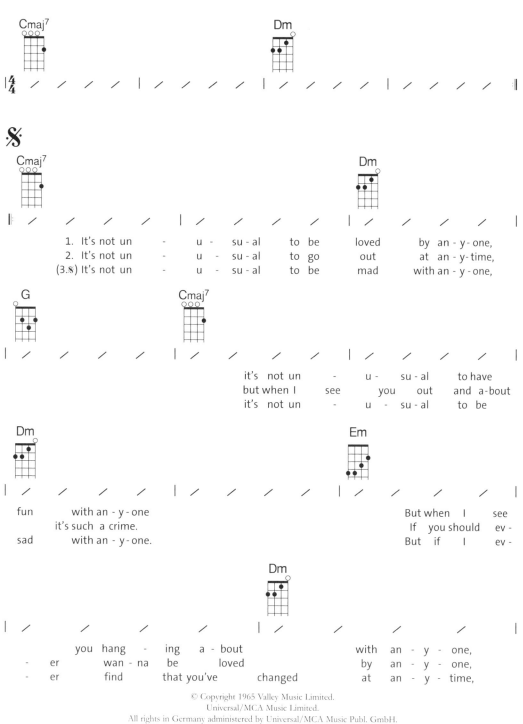

1. It's not un - u - su - al to be loved by an-y-one,
2. It's not un - u - su - al to go out at an-y-time,
(3.%) It's not un - u - su - al to be mad with an-y-one,

it's not un - u - su - al to have
but when I see you out and a-bout
it's not un - u - su - al to be

fun with an-y-one
it's such a crime.
sad with an-y-one.

But when I see
If you should ev -
But if I ev -

you hang - ing a - bout with an-y-one,
- er wan - na be loved by an-y-one,
- er find that you've changed at an-y-time,

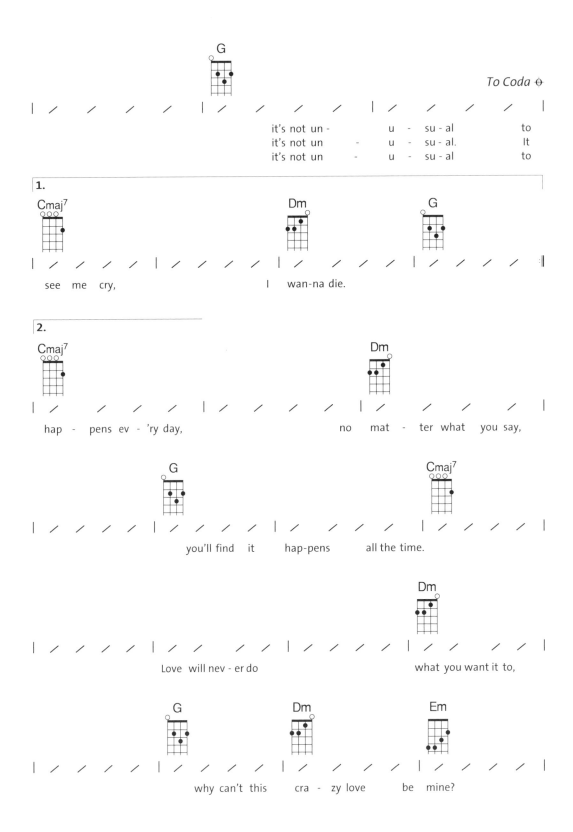

G

To Coda ⊕

| / / / / | / / / / | / / / / |

it's not un -   u - su - al   to
it's not un -   u - su - al.   It
it's not un -   u - su - al   to

1.

Cmaj⁷   Dm   G

| / / / / | / / / / | / / / / |

see   me   cry,   I   wan-na die.

2.

Cmaj⁷   Dm

| / / / / | / / / / | / / / / |

hap - pens ev - 'ry day,   no   mat - ter what   you say,

G   Cmaj⁷

| / / / / | / / / / | / / / / |

you'll find   it   hap-pens   all the time.

Dm

| / / / / | / / / / | / / / / |

Love   will nev - er do   what you want it to,

G   Dm   Em

| / / / / | / / / / | / / / / |

why can't this   cra - zy love   be   mine?

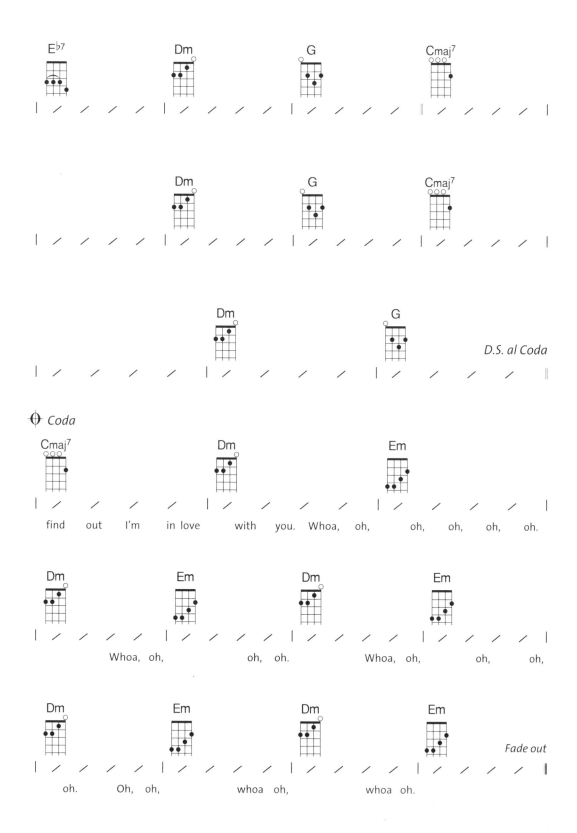

find out I'm in love with you. Whoa, oh, oh, oh, oh, oh.

Whoa, oh, oh, oh. Whoa, oh, oh, oh,

oh. Oh, oh, whoa oh, whoa oh.

peggy sue

Words & Music by Buddy Holly, Norman Petty & Jerry Allison

If you knew Peg-gy Sue, then you'd know why I feel blue a-bout

Peg-gy, my Peg-gy Sue. Oh well, I

love you girl, yes I love you Peg-gy Sue.

Peg-gy Sue, Peg-gy Sue, oh how my heart yearns for you, oh,
2º instrumental

Peg-gy, my Peg-gy Sue. Oh well, I

love you girl, yes I love you Peg-gy Sue.

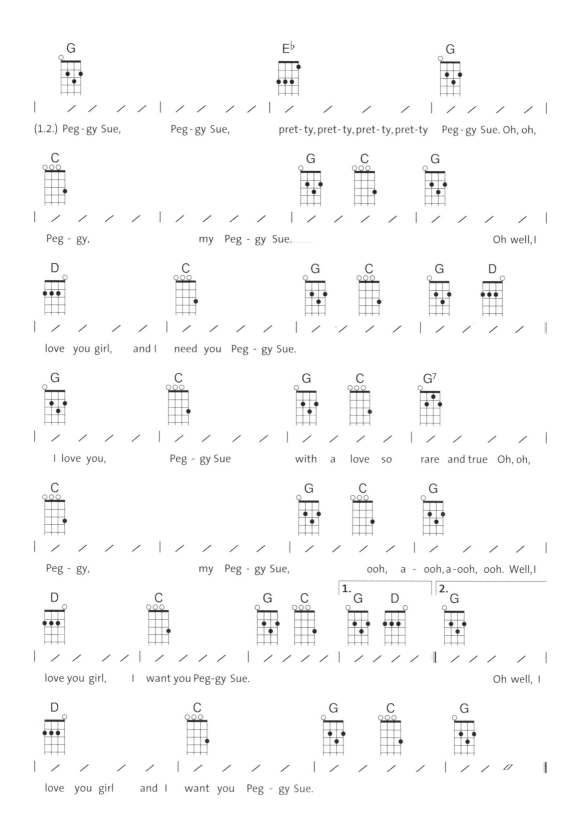

G   Eb   G

| ∕ ∕ ∕ | ∕ ∕ ∕ | ∕ ∕ ∕ | ∕ ∕ ∕ |

(1.2.) Peg - gy Sue, Peg - gy Sue, pret - ty, pret - ty, pret - ty, pret - ty Peg - gy Sue. Oh, oh,

C   G C G

| ∕ ∕ ∕ | ∕ ∕ ∕ | ∕ ∕ ∕ | ∕ ∕ ∕ |

Peg - gy,   my Peg - gy Sue._____   Oh well, I

D   C   G C G D

| ∕ ∕ ∕ | ∕ ∕ ∕ | ∕ ∕ ∕ | ∕ ∕ ∕ ‖

love you girl, and I need you Peg - gy Sue.

G   C   G C G7

| ∕ ∕ ∕ | ∕ ∕ ∕ | ∕ ∕ ∕ | ∕ ∕ ∕ |

I love you, Peg - gy Sue with a love so rare and true Oh, oh,

C   G C G

| ∕ ∕ ∕ | ∕ ∕ ∕ | ∕ ∕ ∕ | ∕ ∕ ∕ |

Peg - gy,   my Peg - gy Sue, ooh, a - ooh, a - ooh, ooh. Well, I

              1.   **2.**

D   C   G C G D G

| ∕ ∕ ∕ ∕ | ∕ ∕ ∕ ∕ | ∕ ∕ ∕ ∕ | ∕ ∕ ∕ ∕ ‖ ∕ ∕ ∕ |

love you girl, I want you Peg - gy Sue.   Oh well, I

D   C   G C G

| ∕ ∕ ∕ ∕ | ∕ ∕ ∕ ∕ | ∕ ∕ ∕ ∕ | ∕ ∕ ∕∕ ‖

love you girl and I want you Peg - gy Sue.

ride a white swan

Words & Music by Marc Bolan

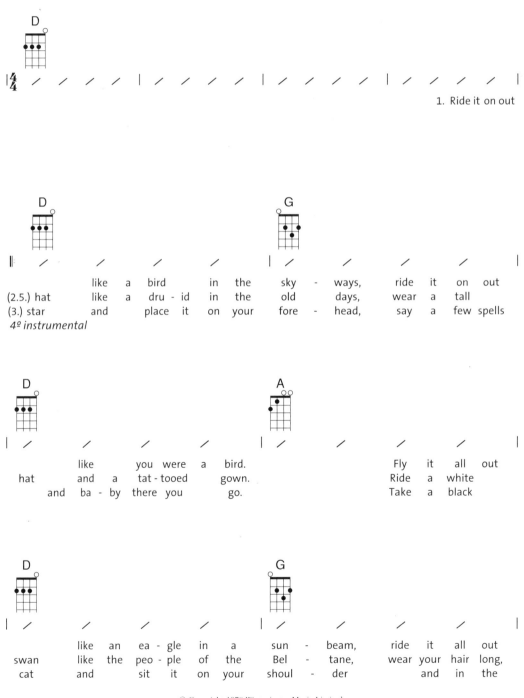

1. Ride it on out

| | like | a | bird | | in the | sky | - ways, | ride | it | on | out |
(2.5.) hat | like | a | dru - id | | in the | old | days, | wear | a | tall |
(3.) star | and | place | it | on your | fore | - head, | say | a | few spells |

4º instrumental

| | like | you were | a | bird. | | | Fly | it | all | out |
hat | and | a | tat - tooed | | gown. | | Ride | a | white |
and | ba - by | there you | | go. | | | Take | a | black |

| | like | an | ea - gle | in | a | sun | - beam, | ride | it | all | out |
swan | like | the | peo - ple | of | the | Bel | - tane, | wear your | hair | long, |
cat | and | sit | it | on your | shoul | - der | | | and | in | the |

D   A   D

/   /   /   /   /   /   /   /

like   you were   a   bird.
babe you can't go   wrong.
morn - ing you'll know all   you   know.   Oh.

/   /   /   /   /   /   /   /

1-5.   **6.**

/   /   /   /   /   /   /   /

2. 5. Wear   a   tall
3. Catch a   bright

/   /   /   /   /   /   /   /

/   /   /   /   /   /   /   /

                                        Da   da

Repeat ad lib. to fade

/ / / /   / / / /   / / / /   / / / /

di di   da,   da da   di di   da.   Da da

singing the blues

Words & Music by Melvin Endsley

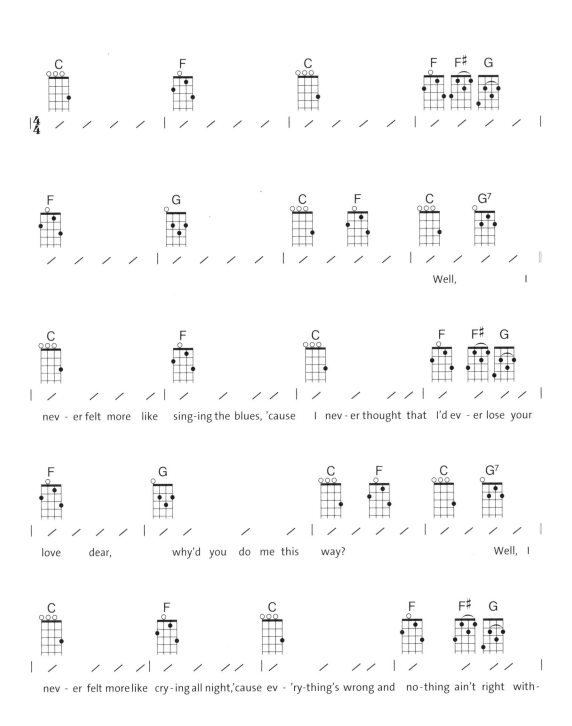

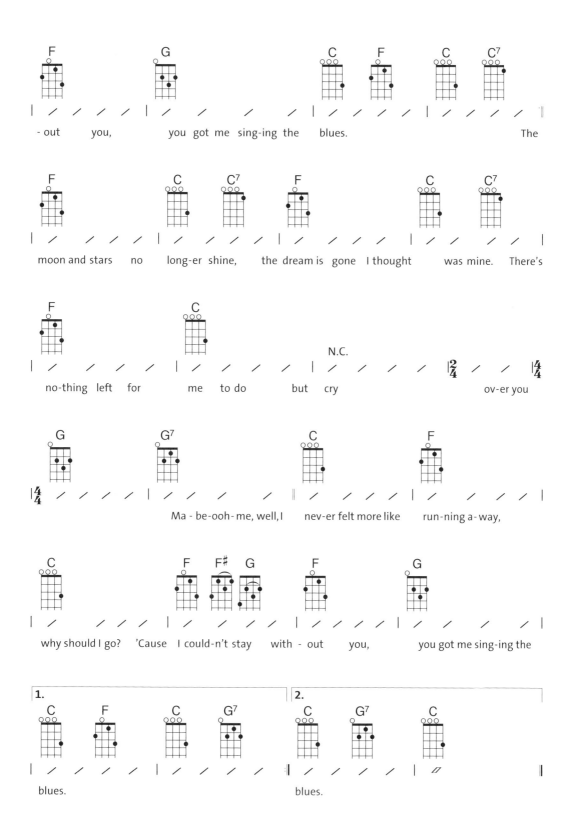

- out   you,   you got me sing-ing the   blues.   The

moon and stars   no   long-er shine,   the dream is gone I thought   was mine.   There's

no-thing left   for   me   to do   but   cry   ov-er you

Ma - be-ooh-me, well, I   nev-er felt more like   run-ning a-way,

why should I go?   'Cause I could-n't stay   with - out   you,   you got me sing-ing the

1. blues.

2. blues.

sloop john b

Traditional

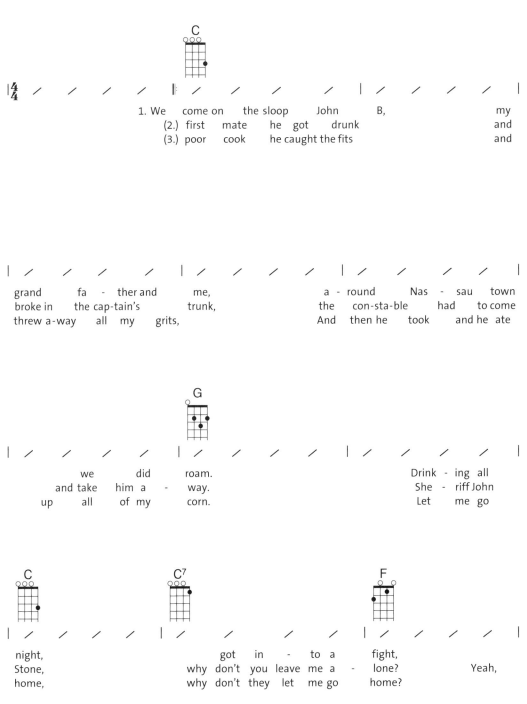

C

1. We   come on   the sloop   John   B,   my
(2.) first   mate   he got   drunk   and
(3.) poor   cook   he caught the fits   and

grand   fa - ther and   me,   a - round   Nas - sau   town
broke in   the cap-tain's   trunk,   the   con-sta-ble   had   to come
threw a-way   all   my   grits,   And   then he   took   and he ate

G

we   did   roam.   Drink - ing all
and take   him a - way.   She - riff John
up   all   of my   corn.   Let   me go

C   C⁷   F

night,   got   in - to a   fight,   Yeah,
Stone,   why don't you leave me a - lone?
home,   why don't they let   me go   home?

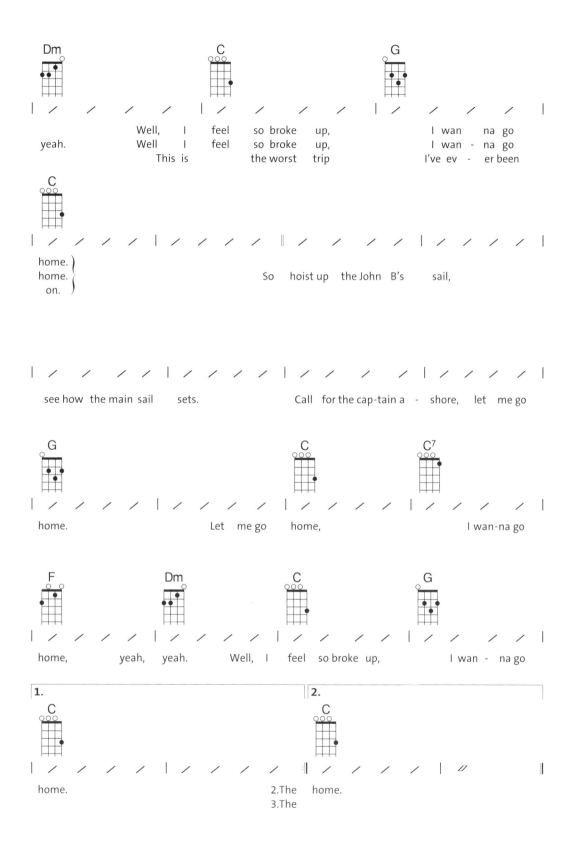

Dm   C   G

| / / / / | / / / / | / / / / |

     Well, I feel so broke up,   I wan na go
 yeah.   Well I feel so broke up,   I wan - na go
      This is   the worst trip   I've ev - er been

C

| / / / / | / / / / ‖ / / / / | / / / / |

 home. ⎫
 home. ⎬
 on. ⎭   So hoist up the John B's sail,

| / / / / | / / / / | / / / / | / / / / |

 see how the main sail sets.   Call for the cap-tain a - shore, let me go

G   C   C⁷

| / / / / | / / / / | / / / / | / / / / |

 home.   Let me go home,   I wan-na go

F   Dm   C   G

| / / / / | / / / / | / / / / | / / / / |

 home,   yeah, yeah.   Well, I feel so broke up,   I wan - na go

1.   **2.**

C   C

| / / / / | / / / / ‖: / / / / | ∥ |

 home.   2.The home.
              3.The

sunny afternoon

Words & Music by Ray Davies

tax - man's ta - ken all   my dough and left me in my   state -ly home,   laz - ing on a
(2.) girl-friend's run off with   my car   and gone back to her   ma and pa,   tell-ing tales of

sun - ny   af - ter-noon.   And I can't   sail   my yacht,   he's ta - ken ev - 'ry
drunk-en-ness   and cru - el-ty.   Now I'm   sit-ting here,   sip - ping at my

thing I've got,   all I've got's this   sun - ny   af - ter-noon.
ice   cold beer,   laz-ing on a   sun-ny   af - ter-noon.

(%) Save me, save me,   save me from this squeeze,   I got a
Help me, help me,   help me sail   a - way,   oh, give me

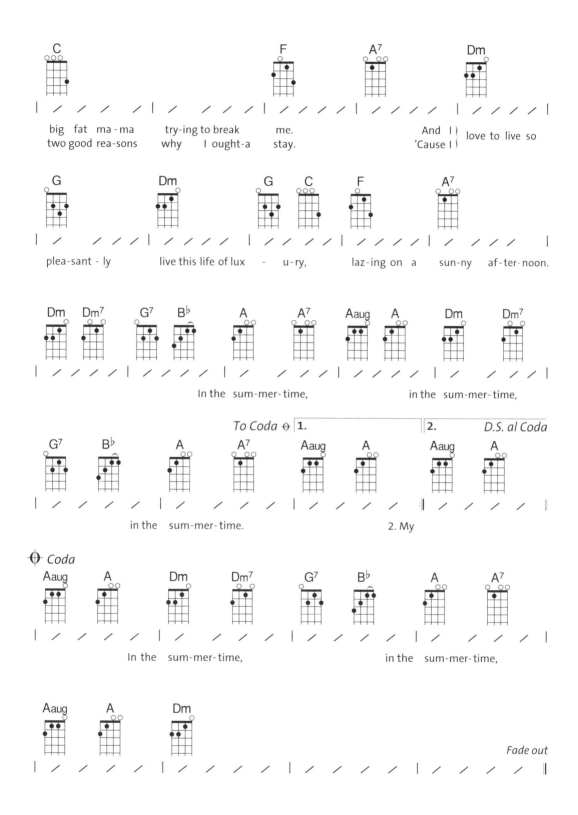

big fat ma-ma try-ing to break me. And I love to live so
two good rea-sons why I ought-a stay. 'Cause I

plea-sant - ly live this life of lux - u-ry, laz-ing on a sun-ny af-ter-noon.

In the sum-mer-time, in the sum-mer-time,

To Coda ⊕ **1.** **2.** *D.S. al Coda*

in the sum-mer-time. 2. My

⊕ *Coda*

In the sum-mer-time, in the sum-mer-time,

Fade out

under the boardwalk

Words & Music by Art Resnick & Kenny Young

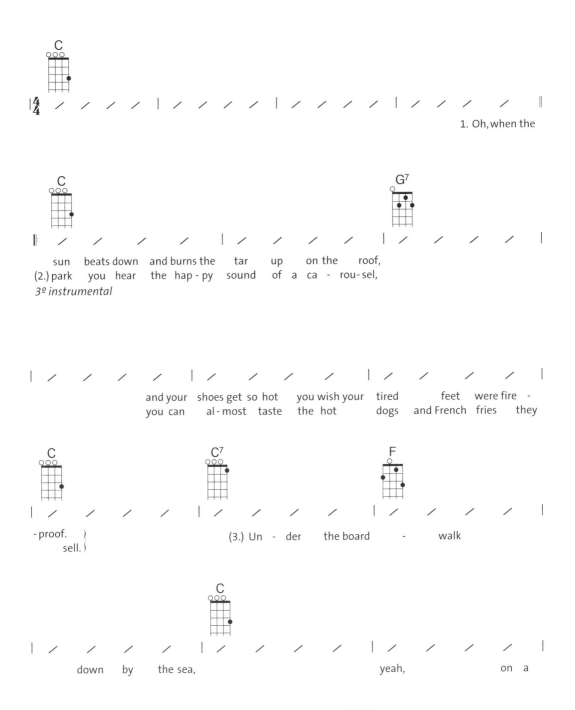

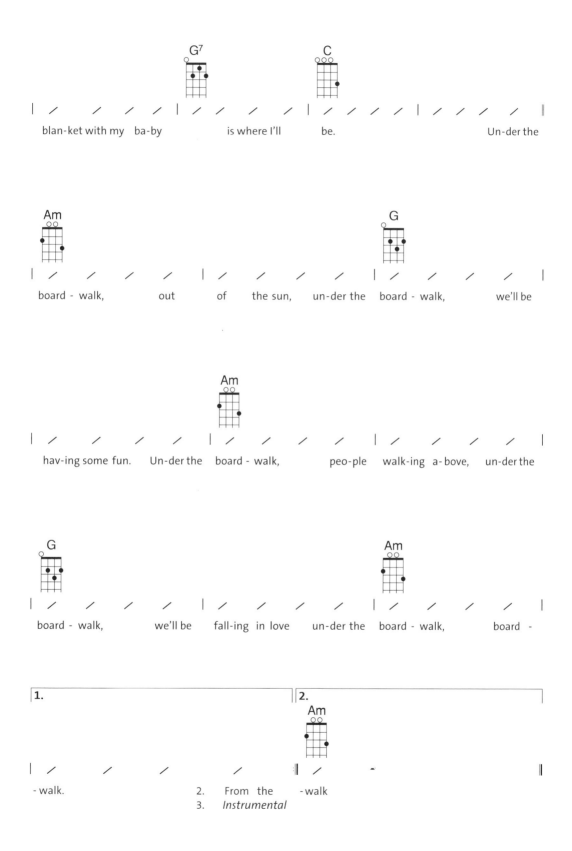

G⁷   C

| /   /   /   / | /   /   /   / | /   /   /   / | /   /   /   / ‖

blan-ket with my ba-by   is where I'll   be.   Un-der the

Am   G

| /   /   /   / | /   /   /   / | /   /   /   / |

board - walk,   out   of   the sun,   un-der the   board - walk,   we'll be

Am

| /   /   /   / | /   /   /   / | /   /   /   / |

hav-ing some fun.   Un-der the   board - walk,   peo-ple   walk-ing a-bove,   un-der the

G   Am

| /   /   /   / | /   /   /   / | /   /   /   / |

board - walk,   we'll be   fall-ing in love   un-der the   board - walk,   board -

1.   **2.**

                                           Am

| /   /   /   / ‖ /   ‖

- walk.   2.   From   the   -walk

                3.   *Instrumental*

you are my sunshine

Words & Music by Jimmie Davis & Charles Mitchell

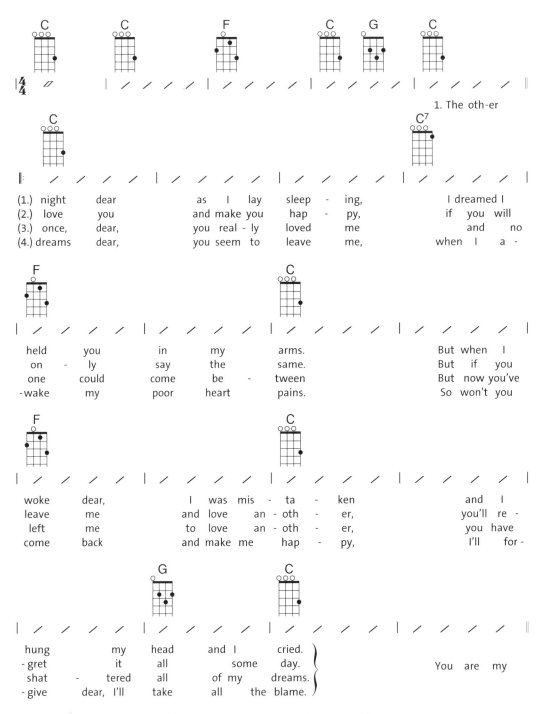

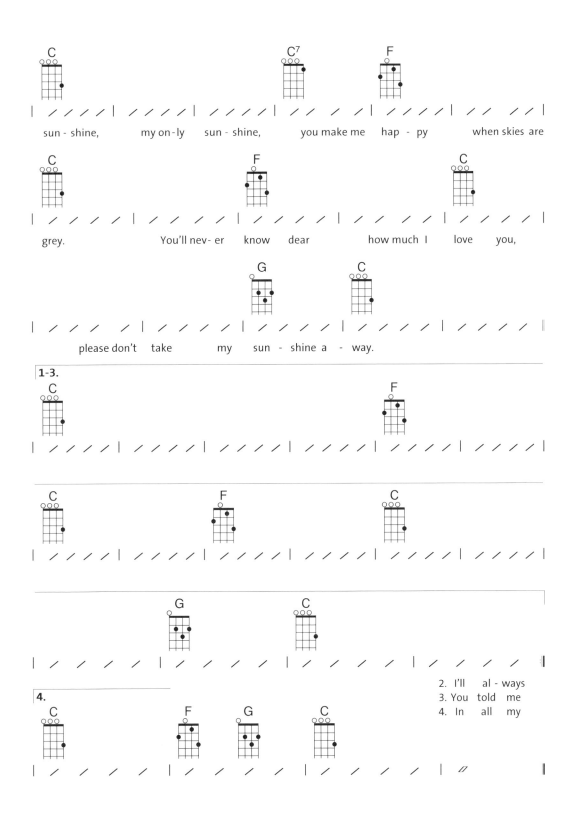

C   C⁷   F
| / / / | / / / | / / / | / / / | / / / | / / / |
sun - shine,   my on-ly   sun - shine,   you make me   hap - py   when skies are

C   F   C
| / / / | / / / | / / / | / / / | / / / | / / / |
grey.   You'll nev- er   know   dear   how much I   love   you,

G   C
| / / / / | / / / / | / / / / | / / / / | / / / / |
please don't   take   my   sun - shine a - way.

1-3.
C   F
| / / / / | / / / / | / / / / | / / / / | / / / / | / / / / |

C   F   C
| / / / / | / / / / | / / / / | / / / / | / / / / | / / / / |

G   C
| / / / / | / / / / | / / / / | / / / / |

2. I'll   al - ways
3. You told   me
4. In   all   my

4.
C   F   G   C
| / / / / | / / / / | / / / / | // |

47